THOUGH SHE BE BUT LITTLE, SHE IS FIERCE

THOUGH SHE BE BUT LITTLE, SHE IS FIERCE

Copyright © Octopus Publishing Group Limited, 2026

All rights reserved.

Compiled by Peggy Jones

No part of this book may be reproduced by any means, nor transmitted, nor translated into a machine language, without the written permission of the publishers.

Condition of Sale
This book is sold subject to the condition that it shall not, by way of trade or otherwise, be lent, resold, hired out or otherwise circulated in any form of binding or cover other than that in which it is published and without a similar condition including this condition being imposed on the subsequent purchaser.

An Hachette UK Company
www.hachette.co.uk

Summersdale Publishers
Part of Octopus Publishing Group Limited
Carmelite House
50 Victoria Embankment
LONDON
EC4Y 0DZ
UK

This FSC® label means that materials and other controlled sources used for the product have been responsibly sourced

www.summersdale.com

The authorized representative in the EEA is Hachette Ireland, 8 Castlecourt Centre, Dublin 15, D15 XTP3, Ireland (email: info@hbgi.ie)

Printed and bound in China

ISBN: 978-1-83799-765-7
eISBN: 978-1-83799-766-4

Substantial discounts on bulk quantities of Summersdale books are available to corporations, professional associations and other organizations. For details contact general enquiries: telephone: +44 (0) 1243 771107 or email: enquiries@summersdale.com.

NOTHING I ACCEPT ABOUT MYSELF CAN BE USED AGAINST ME TO DIMINISH ME.

AUDRE LORDE

SELF-BELIEF DOES EQUATE TO POWER.

GILLIAN ANDERSON

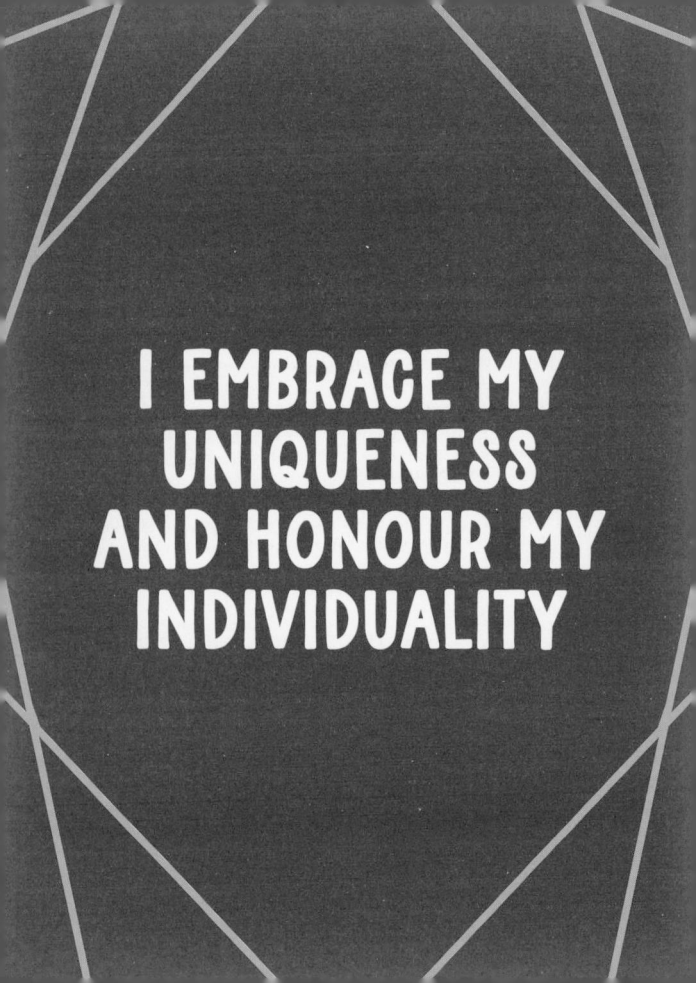

EACH TIME A WOMAN STANDS UP FOR HERSELF, WITHOUT KNOWING IT POSSIBLY, WITHOUT CLAIMING IT, SHE STANDS UP FOR ALL WOMEN.

MAYA ANGELOU

WELL-BEHAVED WOMEN SELDOM MAKE HISTORY.

LAUREL THATCHER ULRICH

I'VE NEVER UNDERESTIMATED MYSELF. **THERE'S NOTHING WRONG WITH BEING AMBITIOUS.**

ANGELA MERKEL

I AM POWERFUL AND CAPABLE

OF ACHIEVING MY DREAMS

IF THEY DON'T GIVE YOU A SEAT AT THE TABLE, BRING A FOLDING CHAIR.

SHIRLEY CHISHOLM

WHAT MAKES ME FEEL THE MOST EMPOWERED IS WHEN I STAND UP FOR MYSELF.

DYLAN MULVANEY

I TRUST MY INTUITION AND FOLLOW ITS GUIDANCE WITH COURAGE

Female resilience is the flame that never dies, turning pain into purpose and lighting the way for those who follow.

GABRIELA SALAS CABRERA

WHEN A WOMAN RISES UP IN GLORY, HER ENERGY IS MAGNETIC AND HER SENSE OF POSSIBILITY CONTAGIOUS.

MARIANNE WILLIAMSON

I WOULD FAIN TEACH WOMEN THAT SELF-DEVELOPMENT IS A HIGHER DUTY THAN SELF-SACRIFICE.

ELIZABETH CADY STANTON

Nothing can shake my confidence

MY COURAGE ALWAYS RISES AT EVERY ATTEMPT TO INTIMIDATE ME.

JANE AUSTEN

ONE CAN
NEVER CONSENT
TO CREEP
WHEN ONE FEELS
AN IMPULSE
TO SOAR.

HELEN KELLER

I AM NO LONGER ACCEPTING THE THINGS I CANNOT CHANGE. I AM CHANGING THE THINGS I CANNOT ACCEPT.

ANGELA DAVIS

MY HEART DREAMS BIG, MY WORDS SPEAK LOUD.

JAZZ JENNINGS

I DO THINGS DIFFERENTLY, BECAUSE I DON'T GO BY A RULE BOOK, **BECAUSE I LEAD FROM THE HEART, NOT THE HEAD.**

DIANA, PRINCESS OF WALES

YOU CAN BE YOU. YOU ARE IN CHARGE OF HOW YOU WANT TO LIVE YOUR LIFE.

NIKKIE DE JAGER

I AM NO ADVOCATE OF PASSIVITY.

LUCRETIA MOTT

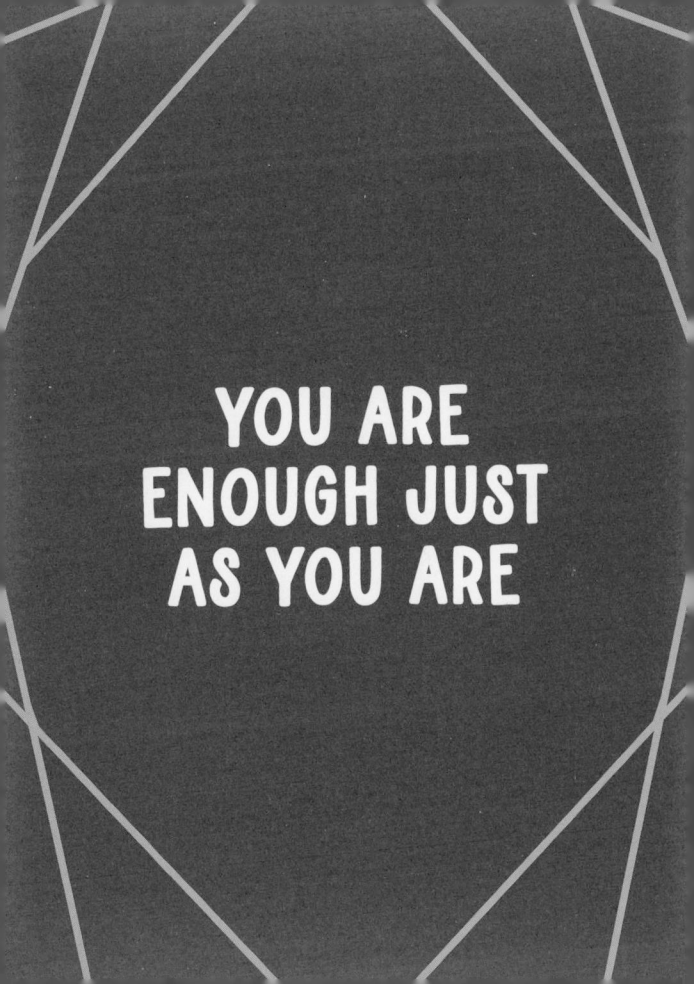

THE FUTURE IS WIDE OPEN AND YOU ARE ABOUT TO CREATE IT BY WHAT YOU DO.

PEMA CHÖDRÖN

NO NEED TO HURRY. NO NEED TO SPARKLE. NO NEED TO BE ANYBODY BUT ONESELF.

VIRGINIA WOOLF

Women are strong and fragile. Women are beautiful and ugly. We are soft-spoken and loud, all at once.

LADY GAGA

> DON'T BUY INTO THE IDEA THAT WOMEN AREN'T STRONG ENOUGH TO DO ANYTHING THEY WANT ON THEIR OWN.
>
> — CHER

EVERYTHING YOU NEED YOU ALREADY POSSESS.

AULI'I CRAVALHO

YOU ARE A FORCE TO BE RECKONED WITH

WHEN YOU'RE FREE, YOUR TRUE CREATIVITY, YOUR TRUE SELF, COMES OUT.

TINA TURNER

SOMETIMES COURAGE IS THE LITTLE VOICE AT THE END OF THE DAY THAT SAYS I'LL TRY AGAIN TOMORROW.

MARY ANNE RADMACHER

REAL POWER IS BORN OF THE HUMILITY AND GRACE OF SISTERHOOD.

KERRY WASHINGTON

WE MUST RESIST THE NOTION THAT THERE IS ONLY ONE WAY TO BE A WOMAN.

WANGARI MAATHAI

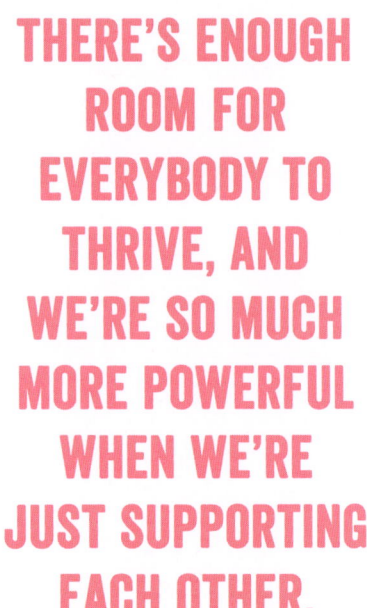

> THERE'S ENOUGH ROOM FOR EVERYBODY TO THRIVE, AND WE'RE SO MUCH MORE POWERFUL WHEN WE'RE JUST SUPPORTING EACH OTHER.
>
> **HAILEY BIEBER**

FEAR CAN'T HOLD YOU BACK

BE YOUR OWN ARTIST, AND ALWAYS BE CONFIDENT IN WHAT YOU'RE DOING.

ARETHA FRANKLIN

I AM A WOMAN AND A WARRIOR. IF YOU THINK I CAN'T BE BOTH, YOU'VE BEEN LIED TO.

ZEYN JOUKHADAR

GIRL POWER IS ABOUT LOVING YOURSELF AND HAVING **CONFIDENCE AND STRENGTH FROM WITHIN.**

NICOLE SCHERZINGER

Be unapologetically you

YOU ARE
WORTHY.
YOU ARE
POWERFUL.
YOU WILL
BREAK
BARRIERS.

HAYLEY KIYOKO

Don't think about making women fit the world – think about making the world fit women.

GLORIA STEINEM

WHAT IF IT'S JUST AROUND THE CORNER? WHAT IF I STOPPED THE DAY BEFORE *THAT* SOMETHING IS MEANT TO HAPPEN?

CHAPPELL ROAN

NEVER LET ANYONE SAY THAT YOU CAN'T DO IT.

SONIA SOTOMAYOR

YES, I'M A FEMINIST, BECAUSE I SEE ALL WOMEN AS SMART, GIFTED AND TOUGH.

ZAHA HADID

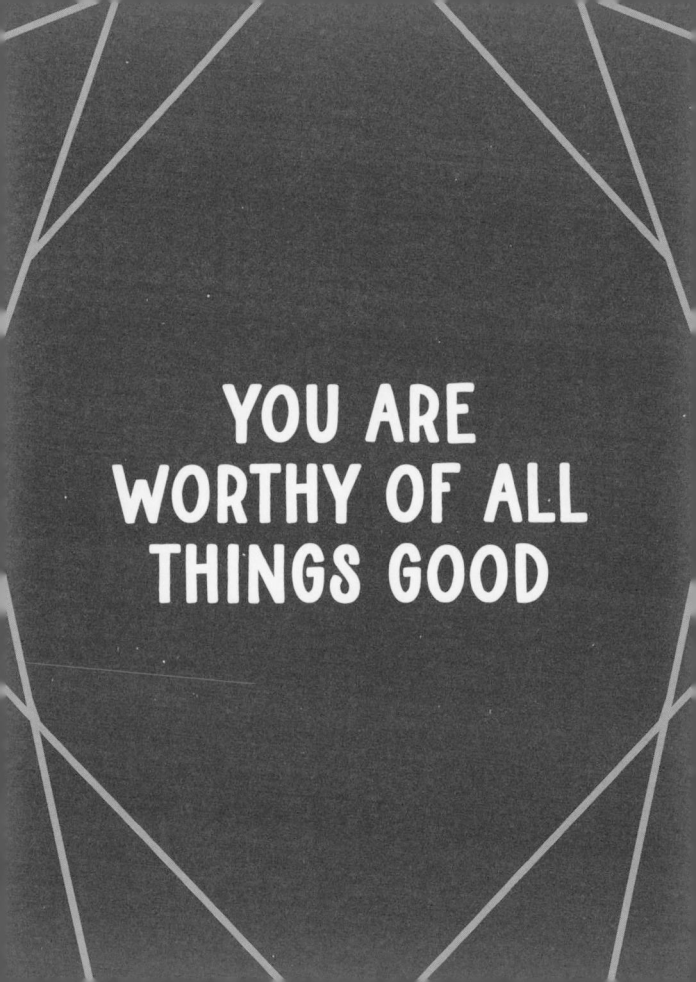

I DO NOT WISH WOMEN TO HAVE POWER OVER MEN; BUT OVER THEMSELVES.

MARY WOLLSTONECRAFT

WOMEN HAVE TO KICK DOWN THE DOORS TO PLACES THEY KNOW THEY ARE NOT INVITED TO.

HANA-RAWHITI MAIPI-CLARKE

MY MOTHER DID NOT RAISE ME TO ASK FOR PERMISSION TO LEAD.

AYANNA PRESSLEY

NEVER BE LIMITED BY OTHER PEOPLE'S LIMITED IMAGINATIONS.

MAE JEMISON

YOU ARE ALLOWED TO BE RADICAL AND HAVE STRONG THOUGHTS THAT OTHERS MIGHT NOT AGREE WITH.

ALICIA KEYS

SELF-BELIEF CAN TAKE YOU ANYWHERE

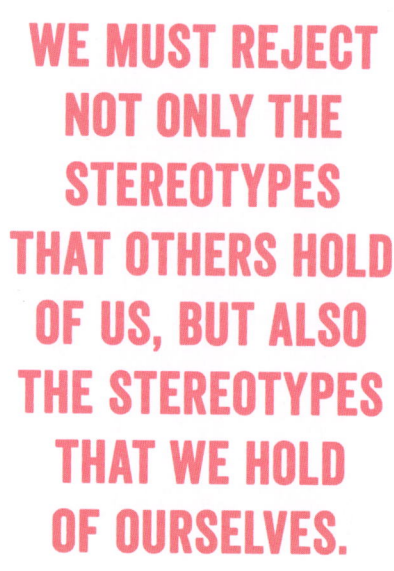

WE MUST REJECT NOT ONLY THE STEREOTYPES THAT OTHERS HOLD OF US, BUT ALSO THE STEREOTYPES THAT WE HOLD OF OURSELVES.

SHIRLEY CHISHOLM

THE MOST RADICAL THING YOU CAN DO IS BE HAPPY.

BETH DITTO

Stand tall in your power

FIND A SENSE OF SELF. WITH THAT, YOU CAN DO ANYTHING ELSE.

ANGELINA JOLIE

I am no bird; and no net ensnares me: I am a free human being with an independent will.

CHARLOTTE BRONTË

> LEARNING HOW TO FALL TEACHES YOU HOW TO LAND. AND LEARNING HOW TO LAND GIVES YOU THE COURAGE TO JUMP HIGH.
>
> — MICHELLE YEOH

SHOW THE WORLD

WHAT YOU CAN DO

WE HAVE ALL A BETTER GUIDE IN OURSELVES, IF WE WOULD ATTEND TO IT, THAN ANY OTHER PERSON CAN BE.

JANE AUSTEN

DON'T LET ANYONE TELL YOU THAT YOU CAN'T DO SOMETHING. ESPECIALLY NOT YOURSELF.

MINDY KALING

YOU CAN MOVE MOUNTAINS

WE ARE WHO
WE KNOW
OURSELVES
TO BE,
AND WE ARE
WHAT WE LOVE.

LAVERNE COX

I AM NOT AFRAID OF STORMS, FOR I AM LEARNING HOW TO SAIL MY SHIP.

LOUISA MAY ALCOTT

I DIDN'T KNOW WHAT I WANTED TO DO, BUT I ALWAYS KNEW THE WOMAN I WANTED TO BE.

DIANE VON FURSTENBERG

BOLD, BRAVE AND UNSTOPPABLE

THERE IS NOTHING A WOMAN CANNOT DO.

ZAKIA KHUDADADI

FEMINISM ISN'T ABOUT MAKING WOMEN STRONG. WOMEN ARE ALREADY STRONG. IT'S ABOUT CHANGING THE WAY THE WORLD PERCEIVES THAT STRENGTH.

G.D. ANDERSON

I LOVE TO SEE PEOPLE JUST BEING REGAL IN THEIR OWN SKIN; IT'S JUST WHEN THEY KNOW WHO THEY ARE.

AVA DUVERNAY

RESILIENCE IS ABOUT FINDING THE STRENGTH AND BEAUTY TO FACE TOUGH SITUATIONS HEAD-ON.

ALLYSON FELIX

WHERE THERE IS A WOMAN THERE IS MAGIC.

NTOZAKE SHANGE

LEAVE FEAR BEHIND

If no one gives you encouragement, you have to encourage yourself.

TEGLA LOROUPE

DO NOT LIVE SOMEONE ELSE'S LIFE AND SOMEONE ELSE'S IDEA OF WHAT WOMANHOOD IS. WOMANHOOD IS YOU.

VIOLA DAVIS

Don't let anyone box you in

NO MATTER WHAT HAPPENS, I'M GOING TO KEEP GOING AND NEVER STOP.

MICHAELA JAÉ RODRIGUEZ

ENERGY APPLIED RIGHTLY AND DIRECTED WILL ACCOMPLISH ANYTHING.

NELLIE BLY

NOTHING IS WORTH MORE THAN LAUGHTER. IT IS STRENGTH TO LAUGH AND TO ABANDON ONESELF, TO BE LIGHT.

FRIDA KAHLO

TOGETHER, WOMEN ARE A FOREST ALIVE WITH SPIRIT.

AMANDA GORMAN

YOUR VOICE IS YOUR POWER. DON'T LET ANYONE TAKE IT AWAY.

KAMALA HARRIS

A REALLY STRONG WOMAN ACCEPTS THE WAR SHE WENT THROUGH AND IS ENNOBLED BY HER SCARS.

CARLY SIMON

I'VE ALWAYS BEEN VERY AWARE OF THE INNER ME THAT HAS NOTHING TO DO WITH THE PHYSICAL ME.

ELIZABETH TAYLOR

COURAGE CALLS TO COURAGE EVERYWHERE, **AND ITS VOICE CANNOT BE DENIED.**

MILLICENT FAWCETT

Let your dreams be bigger than your fears

YOU CAN ACT TO CHANGE AND CONTROL YOUR LIFE. THE PROCESS IS ITS OWN REWARD.

AMELIA EARHART

KEEP GOING. YOU ARE THE CHANGE. THE POWER IS WITHIN US.

ROSE MCGOWAN

Life is a cycle. In the torrid drought, we just survive. In the rainy season, we flourish and grow fruit.

SILVANA SANTOS

ANOTHER WORLD IS NOT ONLY POSSIBLE; SHE IS ON HER WAY. ON A QUIET DAY, I CAN HEAR HER BREATHING.

ARUNDHATI ROY

YOU SHOULD CELEBRATE WHO YOU ARE NOW, WHERE YOU'RE GOING, AND WHERE YOU'VE BEEN.

TAYLOR SWIFT

BE THE CHANGE

YOU WANT TO SEE

WE MUST HAVE PERSEVERANCE AND ABOVE ALL CONFIDENCE IN OURSELVES.

MARIE CURIE

ONLY YOU
KNOW WHAT
YOU CAN
ACCOMPLISH,
AND WHAT
YOU'RE
CAPABLE OF.

JENNIFER LOPEZ

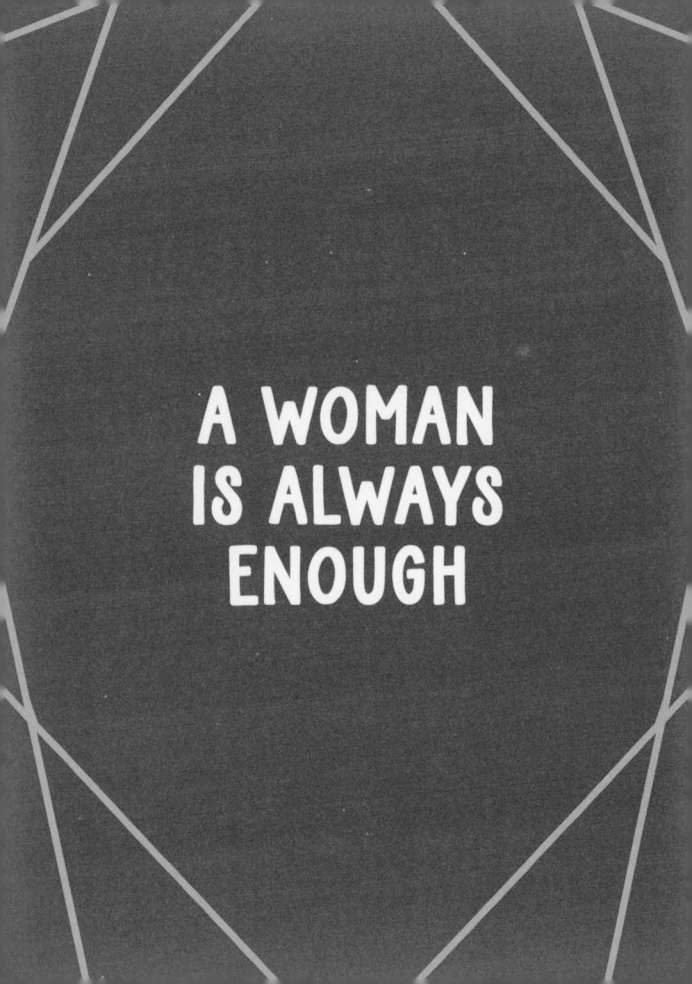

JUST REACH FOR THE STARS AND BACK YOURSELF.

KEELY HODGKINSON

DON'T YOU EVER, EVER GIVE UP ON YOU.

SHERYL LEE RALPH

I WANT TO DISCOURAGE YOU FROM CHOOSING ANYTHING OR MAKING ANY DECISION SIMPLY BECAUSE IT IS SAFE. THINGS OF VALUE SELDOM ARE.

TONI MORRISON

I BELONG TO MYSELF AND I ALWAYS SHALL.

BENAZIR BHUTTO

FACE YOUR FEARS; LIVE YOUR PASSIONS, **BE DEDICATED TO YOUR TRUTH.**

BILLIE JEAN KING

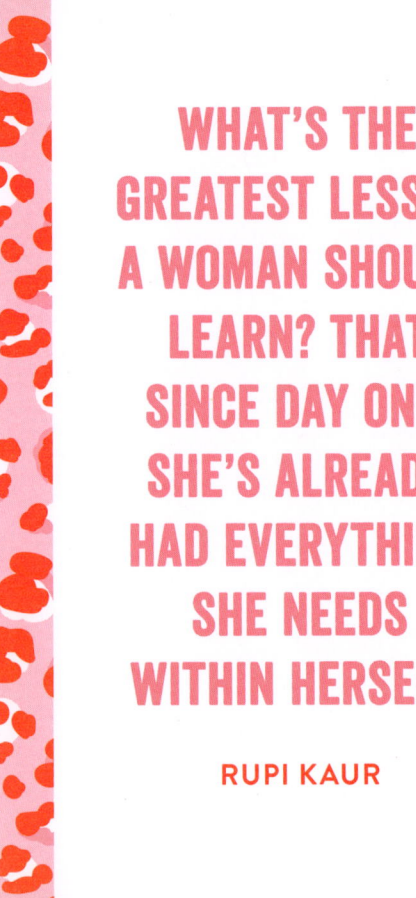

YOU CAN'T LET ANYONE TELL YOU WHAT YOUR BEST IS. YOU KNOW WHAT YOUR BEST IS.

BEYONCÉ KNOWLES

The main thing you need to do is put one foot in front of the other and just keep going.

EMMA CORRIN

WOMAN MUST NOT DEPEND UPON THE PROTECTION OF MAN, BUT MUST BE TAUGHT TO PROTECT HERSELF.

SUSAN B. ANTHONY

THERE IS GREAT VALUE IN BEING FEARLESS.

DIANE KEATON

DON'T GIVE UP TRYING TO DO WHAT YOU REALLY WANT TO DO.

ELLA FITZGERALD

WHEN ONE'S MIND IS MADE UP, THIS DIMINISHES FEAR; KNOWING WHAT MUST BE DONE DOES AWAY WITH FEAR.

ROSA PARKS

DO WHAT YOU'RE DOING NOW. YOU'RE DOING YOUR BEST, YOU'RE GONNA MAKE MISTAKES. DON'T BE SO HARD ON YOURSELF.

MILLIE BOBBY BROWN

Keep dreaming, keep doing

I WANT EVERY GIRL TO KNOW THAT HER VOICE CAN CHANGE THE WORLD.

MALALA YOUSAFZAI

THEY'LL TELL YOU
YOU'RE TOO LOUD –
THAT YOU NEED
TO WAIT YOUR
TURN AND ASK
THE RIGHT PEOPLE
FOR PERMISSION.
DO IT ANYWAY.

ALEXANDRIA
OCASIO-CORTEZ

WEAR YOUR STRENGTH ON YOUR SLEEVE

EVERY WOMAN'S SUCCESS SHOULD BE AN INSPIRATION TO ANOTHER.

SERENA WILLIAMS

BE CONFIDENT, BECAUSE BEING CONFIDENT MEANS BEING HAPPY, **BEING POSITIVE AND ALSO BEING KIND TO OTHER PEOPLE.**

LAURIE HERNANDEZ

I THINK THE KEY IS FOR WOMEN NOT TO SET ANY LIMITS.

MARTINA NAVRATILOVA

IN A WORLD
THAT WANTS
WOMEN TO
WHISPER,
I CHOOSE
TO YELL.

LUVVIE AJAYI JONES

Don't wait around for other people to be happy for you. Any happiness you get you've got to make yourself.

ALICE WALKER

Choose adventure over comfort

> WHAT WOULD HAPPEN IF WE WERE ALL BRAVE ENOUGH TO BE A LITTLE BIT MORE AMBITIOUS? I THINK THE WORLD WOULD CHANGE.
>
> — REESE WITHERSPOON

> YOU WON'T BE HAPPY, WHATEVER YOU DO, UNLESS YOU'RE COMFORTABLE WITH YOUR OWN CONSCIENCE.
>
> LUCILLE BALL

WOMAN MUST NOT ACCEPT; SHE MUST CHALLENGE.

MARGARET SANGER

IF YOU'RE COMFORTABLE WITH YOURSELF AND KNOW YOURSELF, YOU'RE GOING TO SHINE AND RADIATE.

DOLLY PARTON

IT TAKES A CERTAIN GRACE, STRENGTH, INTELLIGENCE, FEARLESSNESS, AND THE NERVE TO NEVER TAKE NO FOR AN ANSWER.

RIHANNA

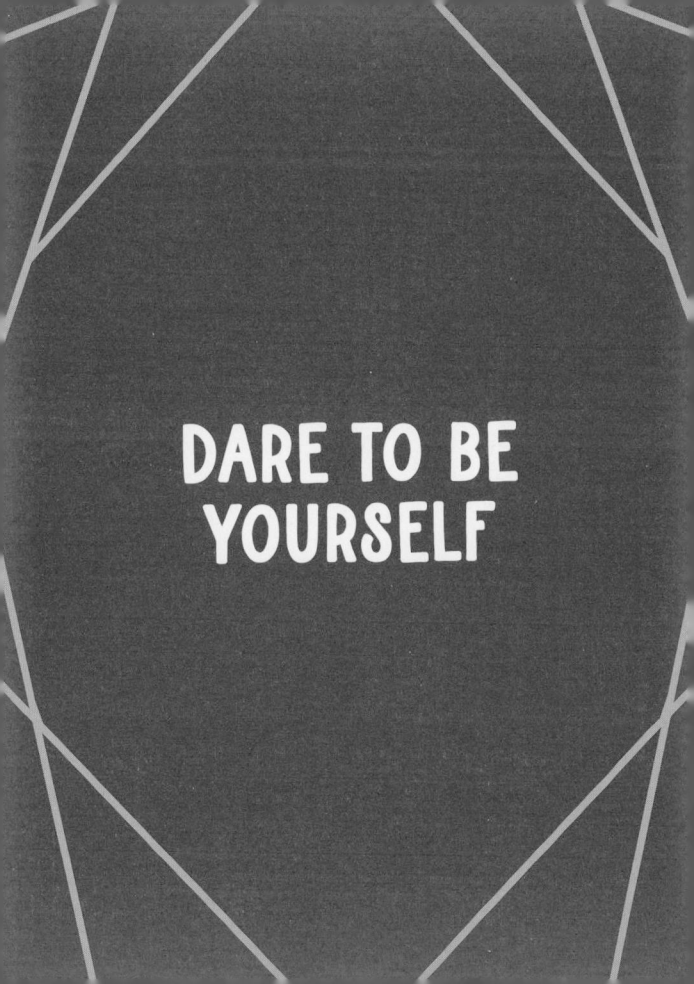

COURAGE IS LIKE A MUSCLE.

WE STRENGTHEN IT BY USE.

RUTH GORDON

IF YOU TRULY POUR YOUR HEART INTO WHAT YOU BELIEVE IN, EVEN IF IT MAKES YOU VULNERABLE, AMAZING THINGS CAN AND WILL HAPPEN.

EMMA WATSON

IF YOU DON'T SEE A CLEAR PATH FOR WHAT YOU WANT, SOMETIMES YOU HAVE TO MAKE IT YOURSELF.

MINDY KALING

You are an infinite well of power

IF YOU KEEP
DREAMING BIG
AND WORKING
TOWARD THOSE
DREAMS,
YOU'LL SEE THEM
COME TRUE.

CYNTHIA ERIVO

YOU BETTER NOT COMPROMISE YOURSELF. IT'S ALL YOU GOT.

JANIS JOPLIN

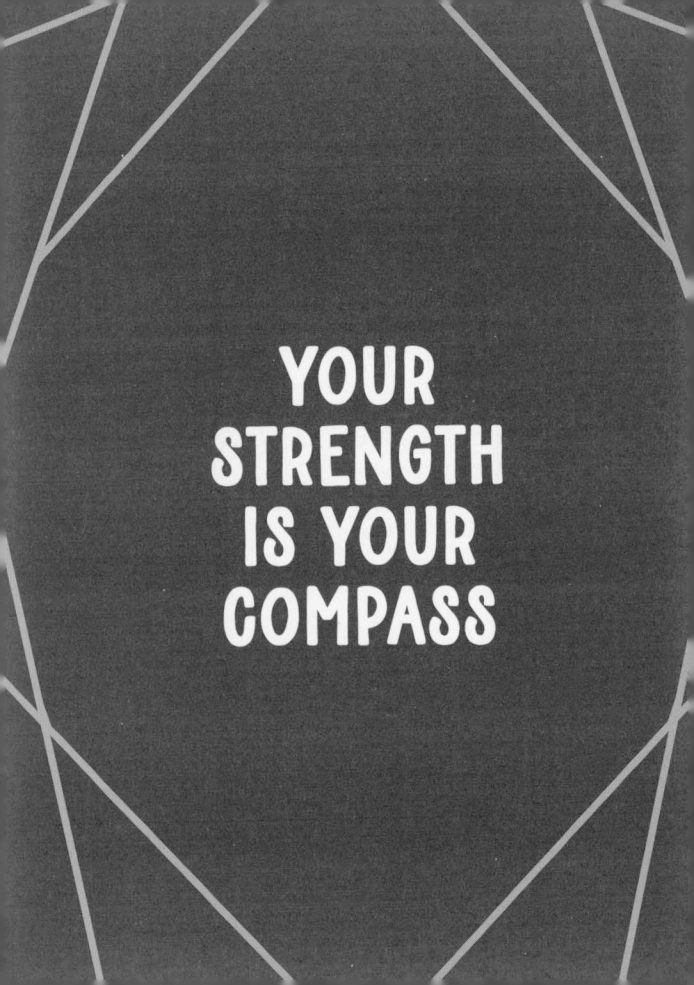

I AM MY OWN EXPERIMENT. I AM MY OWN WORK OF ART.

MADONNA

You can show more of the reality of yourself instead of hiding behind a mask for fear of revealing too much.

BETTY FRIEDAN

THE ONLY COURAGE YOU EVER NEED IS THE COURAGE TO FULFILL THE DREAMS OF YOUR OWN LIFE.

OPRAH WINFREY

WHEN YOU'RE LOUD,

THE WORLD LISTENS

EACH WOMAN CARRIES WITHIN HER A FORCE FOR TRANSFORMATION. MY MESSAGE IS SIMPLE: FIND THAT FORCE, NURTURE IT, AND LET IT SHINE UNAPOLOGETICALLY.

PATRICIA SCOTLAND

FEEL FREE TO CALL THE SHOTS.

RAYE

SILENCE IS NO LONGER AN OPTION.
I AM NOT GOING ANYWHERE.

IMANE KHELIF

STRONG WOMEN DON'T HAVE "ATTITUDES", WE HAVE STANDARDS.

MARILYN MONROE

YOU GAIN STRENGTH, COURAGE AND CONFIDENCE BY EVERY EXPERIENCE IN WHICH YOU REALLY STOP TO LOOK FEAR IN THE FACE.

ELEANOR ROOSEVELT

THOUGH SHE BE BUT LITTLE, SHE IS FIERCE.

WILLIAM SHAKESPEARE

YOU GO GIRL

Empowering Quotes for Awesome Women

ISBN: 978-1-83799-767-1 • Hardback

Every woman deserves to be celebrated.
Embrace your inner strength with this compact
collection of empowering quotes and affirmations,
bursting with advice from an inspiring line-up
of creative, daring and courageous women.

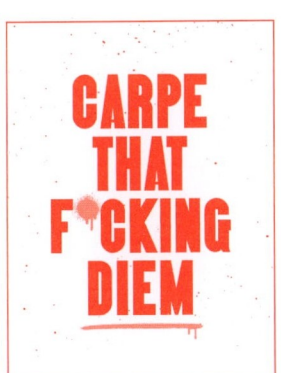

CARPE THAT F*CKING DIEM

Quotes and Mottos for Making the Most of Life

ISBN: 978-1-83799-832-6 • Hardback

Grab life by the horns and go seize the sh*t out of the day with this collection of kick-ass quotations and rousing affirmations. From the wisdom of ancient sages to sound advice from today's superstars, these are words to get you pumped and ready to pursue maximum success and satisfaction!

Have you enjoyed this book?

If so, find us on Facebook at **Summersdale Publishers**, on Twitter/X at **@Summersdale** and on Instagram, TikTok and Bluesky at **@summersdalebooks** and get in touch. We'd love to hear from you!

www.summersdale.com

IMAGE CREDITS

p.3 and throughout © Chief Design/Shutterstock.com

p.4 and throughout – paw print
© Creative icon styles/Shutterstock.com

p.7 and throughout – animal print
© Sinichka/Shutterstock.com

p.10, 14, 24 and throughout © Svetsol/Shutterstock.com

p.12, 17 and throughout – stars
© Tatiana Kuzmina/Shutterstock.com